A Discovery Peephole Book

SEASHORE

by
Richard Powell

TREEHOUSE

Hidden by the seaweed, two eyes peer out. Who could it be?

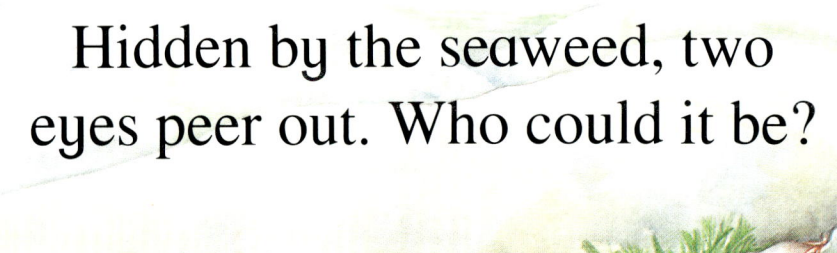

Crabs are ofte
pools. They h
under rocks.
pincers to tea

They eat almo
the bait off fis

And who is that peeking out from a crack in the rocks?

The blenny is a
in rock pools. B
colour to match
which makes

Blennies eat
shellfish, and g

When out of water, this animal looks like a blob of jelly. What is it?

A sea anenome
but its beautif
in the water re
creatures

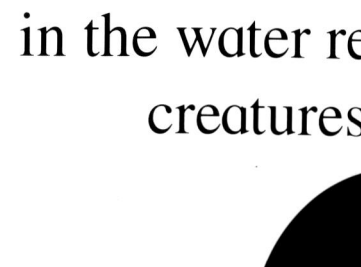

Some big aner
fish and

A shell with legs? What could it be?

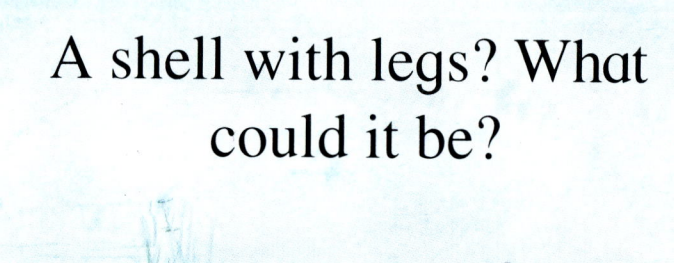

It is a hermit
live in empty
and only co
into a b

Some have a
on the

Clinging to the rocks is a creature with five arms. What is it?

It is a starfis
shellfish such
can open thei
five str

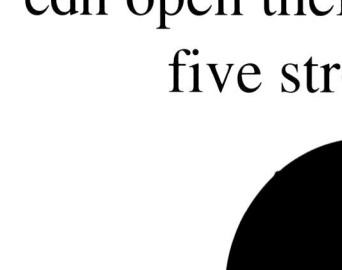

If a starfish
it can grov

What strange creatures are these hiding in the seaweed?

They are shri
the crab. They c
as they dart fro
They are ha

Little shrim
see-throug

A creature that looks like a pin cushion! What could it be?